A
Special Gift

Presented to:

....

From:

....

Date:

....

Stories, Sayings, and Scriptures to Encourage and Inspire

hugs
for
Women

Mary Hollingsworth

Personalized
Scriptures by
LEANN WEISS

HOWARD
PUBLISHING CO.

West Monroe, Louisiana

Our purpose at Howard Publishing is to:

- *Increase faith* in the hearts of growing Christians
- *Inspire holiness* in the lives of believers
- *Instill hope* in the hearts of struggling people everywhere

Because He's coming again!

Hugs for Women © 1998 by Howard Publishing Co., Inc.
All rights reserved. Printed in the United States of America

Published by Howard Publishing Co., Inc.,
3117 North 7th Street, West Monroe, LA 71291-2227

05 06 07 08   25

Written and compiled by Mary Hollingsworth, Shady Oaks Studio,
1507 Shirley Way, Bedford, TX 76022

Paraphrased Scriptures © 2000 LeAnn Weiss, 3006 Brandywine Dr.,
Orlando, FL 32806; 407-898-4410

Interior Design by LinDee Loveland
Edited by Janet Reed

Library of Congress Cataloging-in Publication Data

Hollingsworth, Mary, 1947–
    Hugs for women : stories, sayings, and scriptures to encourage
and inspire / stories by Mary Hollingsworth ; personalized scriptures by LeAnn Weiss.
        p.   cm.
    ISBN 1-878990-81-0
    1. Women—Religious life.   I. Weiss, LeAnn.   II. Title.
BV4527.H655 1998
242' .643—dc21   97-49614

contents

1

Yyou are

Wwoman

1

I have

you ric

every w

hat you

be gene

I have made you rich in every way so that you can be generous on every occasion. Your generosity results in thanksgiving to God.

Love,
Your God of Riches in Glory

2 Corinthians 9:11

Do you ever get tired of being a woman? Do you sometimes wish you could just be somebody else for a few days?

When you see mountains of laundry, a list of errands as long as your arm, and a stack of paperwork that needed attention yesterday, would you just like to scream and run out the door? "Here, honey, you be the woman this week. Bye!"

And then you would escape to the freedom of no responsibilities – lunch with a friend at that new bistro down the street and a few hours surfing the net just for fun at www.calm. Peace. Quiet. A leisurely stroll along the riverbank, an hour-long bubble bath with a good book and no interruptions, shopping, and a huge helping of death-by-chocolate dessert (without thinking about the calories). No phones. No beepers. No problems to solve. No PMS. No stress. Ahhhhh . . .

Still, think about it. After a few days with no responsibilities, wouldn't you miss the chubby little arms that wrap tightly around your neck? Wouldn't you miss the secret smile that your husband has just for you? Wouldn't you miss your boss's open admiration for the excellent work you do? Wouldn't you miss being "the one in charge" of the community's Fourth of July event? Wouldn't you miss just being you — an amazing, creative, needed, capable, blessed, and loved woman?

God created you as a woman on purpose. It was no accident, no mistake. He specifically made you to fill a role in this life. He endowed you with carefully chosen gifts and abilities to enable you to fill that important role successfully. He depends on you to be who you were created to be.

I recently discovered that the Old Testament Hebrew word for "Holy Spirit" is a feminine word. And I thought, *Of course! The comforter. The guide. The one who teaches and leads. God created woman after the feminine side of his image. We are the gentle spirit of joy and peace that blesses those around us.*

Celebrate! You are God's extended feminine presence in this world. Without you, the world would have an incomplete picture of God. You are woman . . . God's woman.

5

They talk about a woman's sphere

As though it had a limit;

There's not a task to mankind given,

There's not a blessing or a woe,

There's not a whispered "yes" or "no,"

There's not a life, there's not a birth

That has feather's weight of worth

Without a woman in it.

Speaker's Sourcebook

She wandered into their lives,

touched them gently,

and then selflessly wandered away,

never to be seen by them again.

She had amazed them with her

kindness and generosity.

And yet, she was no bigger-than-life heroine.

She was just an ordinary woman —

a woman who gave up her own dream

for someone else's.

the dream

She pulled into town one cool, autumn afternoon, driving slowly down the main street. She stopped at the only traffic light before parking in front of the grocery store. Carolyn bought bread, bologna, cheese, pickles, chips, and a Coke. Then she climbed back into her car and drove to the edge of town where she noticed a small park in a grove of elm trees. She stopped there to eat her picnic lunch.

As she dumped her trash into the metal barrel, Carolyn caught her breath. There it was! At long last, after her five-year search, she had found it. Tucked into a secluded spot in the woods stood a little cottage – the one she had always imagined as her writing retreat. A dirt path led from the park to the cottage's front gate.

Walking slowly along the path, Carolyn tried to soak up every detail around the small, deserted building. Fallen elm leaves crunched beneath her feet as she walked reverently through the white-picket gate and up the old brick walk to the front porch. She tried the front door, and it opened without resistance. A quick inspec-

10

tion made her heart beat a little faster with anticipation. It was the perfect place for a well-known author to find the anonymity and solitude necessary for writing.

Returning to the front porch, Carolyn sat down in the swing and began to push it gently back and forth, back and forth. Its metal chain squeaked softly in rhythm with her thoughts: *It needs new paint, and the shingles on the roof have to be replaced. The roses need to be pruned, and the lawn has to be mowed. But mostly, it needs someone to live in it, love it, care for it. It's perfect! I wonder why it's empty. Is it for sale?*

11

A sudden impulse sent Carolyn running back to her car. She drove quickly back into town and found the local real estate office. When she asked about the little cottage, she learned that it had been repossessed by the bank; its former owners couldn't pay the back taxes. All she had to do was pay the taxes, and it was hers . . . which is exactly what Carolyn did.

Handing her the key and deed to her new writing retreat, the real estate agent told her about a local fix-it man named Henry. He could help her make the needed repairs. Carolyn stopped to talk to him on her way back to the cottage and arranged for him to begin work the next day.

12

By mid-December all the repairs had been made. The roof no longer leaked, the cottage had a fresh coat of pale-yellow paint and forest-green shutters, the lawn had a manicured look, and Carolyn had added some homey touches inside. It was the perfect haven for writing. Soon she could sit down at her desk overlooking the goldfish pond and begin working on her next novel.

One chilly afternoon as Carolyn swept the leaves off the front porch, she heard a small voice say, "Hello." Looking up, she saw a little red-haired girl swinging on the front gate.

"Well, hello," said Carolyn with a smile. "What's your name?"

"Jenny. What's yours?"

"Carolyn."

"How do you like the house?" the little visitor asked.

"I *love* it. It's just what I've always wanted."

"We liked it too," said Jenny. "It looks nice with the new paint."

13

Carolyn stopped sweeping. "Thanks. Did you live here?"

"Yes, until my daddy died. Then we had to move."

"Where do you live now?" Carolyn asked with concern.

"In the shelter downtown."

Carolyn put down her broom and walked out to the gate. "I'm sorry your daddy died. What happened?"

"He was sick for a long time, and he couldn't work. The doctors couldn't make him well. They said he had something called leukemia. He died last year, just before Christmas. Then the bank told Mama that we'd have to move. She cried a lot after that."

"I'm so sorry, Jenny. Say, I've got some lemonade inside. Would you like some?"

14

"Thanks, but I have to go now. My mom will be worried about me. I have to take care of my baby brother while she cooks dinner at the shelter. Maybe I'll come back sometime."

"Please do," Carolyn said quietly as Jenny walked away, glancing back at the little cottage wistfully two or three times before she was out of sight.

Suddenly Carolyn's happy little cottage – her dream – seemed sad and lonely. In her mind she could see Jenny and her family playing in the yard. She could imagine the smell of homemade bread baking in the small kitchen. She could hear the sounds of laughter that now seemed to echo eerily in the trees. And she knew what she had to do.

15

On Christmas Eve Henry, dressed up in a Santa Claus suit, rang the bell at the downtown shelter. He entered with a happy, "Ho Ho Ho!" and started giving presents to all the children. He handed Jenny a special doll with red hair just like hers, and he had a big, blue rubber ball for Jenny's baby brother.

The last thing in Santa's sack was an ordinary white envelope. He walked quietly over to Jenny's mother and said, "Sarah, this is for you." Looking quizzically at him, Sarah took the envelope and tore open the sealed flap. When she removed a piece of paper from the envelope, a key fell into her lap. She recognized it immediately. When she looked at the paper, she realized it was

16

the deed to the cottage – with *her* name on it – marked "Paid in Full."

Tears welled up in her eyes as she pulled out the second piece of paper. The light blue note read, "Please come home. I miss you. Merry Christmas." It was signed, "The Cottage by the Park."

She wandered into their lives, touched them gently, and then selflessly wandered away, never to be seen by them again. She had amazed them with her kindness and generosity. And yet, she was no bigger-than-life heroine. She was just an ordinary woman – a woman who gave up her own dream for someone else's. She was a woman probably very much like you.

17

Reflections . . .

18

you are

amazing

My dau
you are
vorkma
created
Christ J

M

y daughter, you
are my workmanship, created in
Christ Jesus to do good works.
I've already prepared you in
advance for everything I've
planned especially for you to do.

Love,

Your God of Purpose

Ephesians 2:10

A woman is not just a person; she's a miracle! Like a cosmic shape-shifter of *Star Trek,* she can transform into anything she needs to be in an instant.

She turns into a nurse at the sight of a scrape of a scratch; in larger emergencies, she's instantly a paramedic.

When trouble comes or the enemy attacks, she becomes the fortress behind which the whole family – even Dad – huddles for protection.

Or she snaps her fingers and changes into a Little League coach, a Girl Scout leader, a homeroom mother, a corporate executive, a financier, a Sunday school teacher, a playmate, a seamstress, a play director, or a volunteer for the March of Dimes.

She is, all in the same day, a cook, a taxi driver, a boardroom presenter, a maid, a politician, and a referee.

She can be a shrewd merchant at a garage sale, an orator at PTA, a delightful storyteller at the daycare center, and a military genius in organizing the neighborhood against crime.

And, at the wave of a wand, she emerges as Cinderella ready for the ball and waltzes out the door on the arm of her prince charming.

In addition, she is often the spiritual heart of the home – guiding, encouraging, leading, teaching, praying. She is God's hands and feet, his laughter and joy, his tears and sorrow. She is the heart of God personified.

There's no doubt about it – a woman is not just a person; she's a miracle!

23

A nation is not conquered until

the hearts of its women are

on the ground.

Then it is done,

no matter how brave its warriors

nor how strong their weapons.

❧

Cheyenne Proverb

Dorothy was an amazing woman,

like so many other women I've known.

Her determination and faith in God

carried her through to her goal.

the goal

1965. We were in the middle of the Vietnam War. I was a junior in high school in a small rural community in central Texas. And life on this side of the water was good . . . for most of us.

In the class ahead of me – the envied graduating class – was a young man named Robby, a big bruiser and captain of the football team. He had classic good looks, too, which didn't make the girls like him any less. And he studied hard, which didn't make the teachers like him any less. All in all, Robby was a fine man – responsible, dependable, and courageous.

Robby was the only son of Dorothy, a widow who was dying of cancer. Every day at lunchtime and immediately after school, Robby went home to take care of his mom. Although frail, Dorothy always wore a bright smile. And she was so proud of Robby.

28

Dorothy dreamed of living long enough to see Robby graduate from high school. "After that," she said, "I can rest easy." The doctors said she would never make it to the end of May; the cancer had spread through-out her body and continued to grow rapidly. But she always answered with confidence,

"Oh, yes, I'll make it. I *have* to make it. I want to be there for Robby."

The spring went by slowly for Dorothy. She endured a lot of pain, and the days dragged while Robby was at school. He wanted to stay home with her, but she wouldn't hear of it. She wanted to see him graduate and be ready to face the world on his own. When word of her goal got around the small town, several women began taking turns sitting with Dorothy during the day so Robby could go to school without worrying about her so much. Dorothy's goal became the entire town's goal.

29

Dorothy enjoyed helping Robby choose his senior ring, and together they addressed and sent out his graduation announcements. She loved all the preparations for the big day. And she made plans to attend herself, in spite of the warnings from her doctors and friends.

Because the town was so small – 982 citizens in all – graduation ceremonies rotated between the three largest churches. In 1965 the ceremony would take place in the church where my father was the minister, and he was the scheduled commencement speaker.

30

When May 28 finally arrived, parents, teachers, students, and other friends from the community filled the church building. The nineteen seniors lined up excitedly in the foyer wearing their black robes and caps with gold-and-white tassels. At the arranged cue from the assistant principal, they marched in and filled the first three rows of the church. My dad, the superintendent of schools, and the high school principal entered from the front and took their appointed places on the podium. We were ready to begin.

At that moment, the doors at the back were opened, and two ambulance attendants rolled Dorothy in on a stretcher. A hush fell over the gathering. The raised back of the stretcher supported Dorothy in a semi-sitting position, and she wore a beautiful new aqua-colored dress. Her hair had been professionally done, and her makeup was perfect. She looked beautiful. A brilliant smile lit up her face as she spotted Robby among the seniors, sitting next to the center aisle.

31

The attendants rolled the stretcher down the aisle and positioned Dorothy next to her son, facing the podium so she could see and hear everything. Robby reached out and took her hand as the speeches began.

The rest of the ceremony proceeded normally, except that we could not take our eyes off Dorothy and Robby. It was a bittersweet experience for everyone but Dorothy, who looked ecstatic the entire time.

32

At the end of the ceremony, in traditional senior fashion, the graduates cheered and threw their caps into the air. Dorothy cheered and clapped too. Her dream had come true. Her Robby had graduated, and she had lived to see it. No one had dry eyes.

Three days later, Dorothy died. She had held out as long as she needed to. She knew she could rest now, and so she did. She was buried in her beautiful new aqua dress.

Unknown to Dorothy, Robby had received his draft notice two weeks earlier and had enlisted in the marines. A week after his mother died, Robby left for boot camp and then Vietnam. In less than a year, Robby died in action and joined his mother.

Dorothy was an amazing woman, like so many other women I've known. Her determination and faith in God carried her through to her goal. I think of her often, and I know that we can all reach our goals with strong determination and great faith. And someday, when we have our reached goals, we can also rest easy with the Lord.

33

Reflections . . .

34

_____

_____

_____

_____

_____

_____

_____

_____

_____

_____

_____

_____

_____

you are
creative

Celebrat

uniquen

No one

an do

I've crea

Celebrate your uniqueness! No one else can do what I've created you to do! Use the special gifts and abilities I have given you to serve others and to faithfully administer my amazing grace as only you can.

Love,
Your Lord of Creativity
P.S. When I appoint, I also anoint!

1 Peter 4:10; James 1:17

Most of the women I know would deny that they are creative. What they really mean is they can't sing, paint, act, or write. Therefore, they must not be creative.

Sadly, through the centuries, our primary concept of *creativity* has been confined to the fine arts. What an enormous mistake! It's certainly not a biblical notion, and its negative effect can never be measured.

In truth, every person is creative in one way or another. The Bible is plain: "God created human beings in his image" – the image of the Great Creator – "male and female he created them." Born with his creative genes, we are endowed with his cleverness and ingenuity. We are blessed with his ability to see finished projects in our minds before we even begin them: events, buildings, garments, budgets, families, meals, missions, and yes, paintings, books, compositions, and dramas.

Our task as his children is to find our personal area of giftedness and talent and to use it for him. Perhaps your God-given creativity lies in the area of teaching, parenting, sewing, accounting, administrating, comforting, building, computing, organizing, or landscaping. He may have blessed you as a creative athlete, musician, caregiver, counselor, food preparer, or mechanic.

In his almighty wisdom, God made us to need each other's creativity. We are not self-sufficient but interdependent. I may need your mechanical skill with my car, and you may need my ability to write a résumé. I definitely need my friend Barbara's talent for balancing checkbooks, she needs Charlotte's musical leadership, and Charlotte needs Dr. Russell's veterinary care for her dog, Cricket. I need your creative gift, and you need mine. That's the plan of the Great Creator.

39

Celebrate your creativity! Don't deny your gift or your identity as the child of the Creator. Reach out and touch others with the gift God has chosen to impart through you. And reap the joy!

We are each inspired treasures,

with creative gifts to share.

The world needs your gifts!

❧

Sark

The song of praise from one of God's

creative women had done more good

than any punishment could

have accomplished that day

in the hearts of those wayward men.

Lives had been touched.

Hearts had been changed.

Perhaps even souls had been saved.

the song

It had been a typical Saturday night for the busy San Francisco Police Department. Officers had rounded up more than thirty red-eyed, disheveled men for being drunk and disorderly in local bars, clubs, and alleys. On Sunday morning the thirty-plus offenders stood before the judge to hear their deserved punishment.

Some of the men were old, hardened alcoholics who had been before the judge

on numerous occasions and who had no intention of changing their ways. They knew it, and he knew it. Others – first-time lawbreakers – stood with their heads hung in shame. They couldn't even look into the face of the judge.

After the motley bunch was assembled before the judge, the uniformed escorts retreated behind the railing. Quiet settled over the room, and His Honor was about to begin when a strange thing happened. A beautiful, clear soprano voice pierced the silence with the opening strains of "The Holy City":

Last night I lay a'sleeping,
There came a dream so fair.

44

Last night! For the guilty group in the courtroom, last night had been a disaster . . . a nightmare or a drunken stupor. The contrast of the song and their own experiences couldn't be ignored. It shocked each man to the core of his being. Then the song continued:

> I stood in old Jerusalem,
> Beside the Temple there.

45

The judge paused, unable to proceed while the song echoed through the hallowed halls of justice. He asked one of the policemen who was singing and learned that a former member of a famous opera company was awaiting trial for forgery.

As the song went on, every man in the courtroom was overcome with emotion . . . even the hardened alcoholics. A few men dropped to their knees. One young man tried desperately to control himself but finally collapsed against the wall, buried his face against his folded arms, and sobbed, "Oh mother, mother!"

The young man's sobbing, blended with the stirring melody, cut to the very heart of every man assembled. Eventually, wiping his eyes, one man protested, "Judge, have we got to submit to this? We're here to take our punishment, but this . . ." Then his voice broke, and he began to cry aloud too.

Although it was impossible to continue the business of the court, the judge did not order the singer stopped. Rather, he sat in

silence studying the line of men as the song
rose to its magnificent climax:

> Jerusalem, Jerusalem!
>   Sing, for the night is o'er!
> Hosanna in the highest!
>   Hosanna for evermore!

When the powerful final words had
faded, a hush settled over the solemn courtroom. The wise old judge looked into the
faces of the scoundrels before him – broken,
weeping men. Not one of the offenders had
gone untouched. Their remorse was plain.

After several moments, the judge cleared
the emotion from his throat and quietly
advised the men before him to think about
what they had heard and change their ways.

47

He didn't call individual cases or impose any kind of fine or punishment. No one was sentenced to the workhouse that day. The men were simply dismissed.

The song of praise from one of God's creative women had done more good than any punishment could have accomplished that day in the hearts of those wayward men. Lives had been touched. Hearts had been changed. Perhaps even souls had been saved.

Your creative gift from God might also touch the life and heart of someone around you. God's gifts are powerful, transforming tools, especially when we focus them on reaching out to others with his message of love and grace. Our simple task is to find ways to use our creative gifts, whatever those gifts may be, to praise him.

48

Reflections . . .

49

Reflections . . .

4

Y you are

needed

You are
special a
needed
of the b
of Chris

Y ou are a special and needed part of the body of Christ. Even if you feel weak or insignificant, you are indispensable! I've shaped you with special gifts of service needed for the common good. I've arranged you and gifted you to be needed.

Love,
Your God and Creator

1 Corinthians 12

Those who love you need you in so many different ways, in every area of their lives in which you play a role.

How are you needed?

Your parents need you as a daughter, as a support, as a source of joy. Your siblings need you as a sister, a correspondent, and a partner in family matters.

Your best friend needs you as a listener, as a funmate, as a burden sharer, as an encourager and helper.

If you are married, your husband needs you as a loving wife. He may also need you as a tennis partner, bill payer, confidante, and secret keeper. Your children need you as a mother, as a teacher, as a guide, and as a counselor.

Your church family needs you as a spiritual light, a fellow traveler along the Way, a prayer partner, a spring of hope and faith. And all the other people with whom you have relationships need you in the distinctive roles you fill in their lives.

God needs you too. He endowed you with special abilities to serve in his church and his world. Perhaps he gave you the gift of hearing the soulful cries of his hurting children. Maybe he gave you eyes of compassion that see the desperation in the faces of abused women and children and the sensitive heart that calls you to help them. He may have blessed you with a can-do spirit that inspires others to get involved in projects that look impossible. Or perhaps he infused you with overflowing joy that splashes onto anyone who comes near and urges them onward and upward.

Whatever gifts and abilities he gave you, he needs you to be at work in his world and his kingdom. No one else can do what he designed you for in the same way you can.

55

So many people need you in so many ways, and no one can take your place. No one else can play your role. No one else knows your lines. You are uniquely created to fit in the special you-shaped space God formed in his world. Never wonder if you are needed. The fact that you are here proves it!

Look for a reason

to need people,

and they will need you

in return.

❧

M. Norvel Young

Divine hugs often have human arms —

a best friend's, a mate's, a parent's.

And because they are

God's personified presence,

it's okay to cry in their embrace. . . .

We need him.

No one else will do.

no one else will do

Susan was deaf. Suddenly deaf. She had grown up as a hearing person, but at age twenty-one, she awoke one morning to silence. She had only 10 percent residual hearing left in one ear.

I met Susan at church about two years later. An upbeat, outgoing, happy woman, Susan loved people and loved the Lord. She taught sign language for the hearing impaired at the university across the street from our church building.

A few weeks after coming to the church, Susan announced that she would teach sign language classes at the church for anyone who wanted to learn to speak to the deaf. I enrolled primarily because my mom's sister is deaf, and I had always wanted to be able to speak to her more effectively.

Susan and I spent many long hours together practicing sign language – her teaching, me learning. It was a delightful time of sharing.

Susan told me that when she first became deaf, she was terrified because she could no longer hear Kelli, her three-year-old daughter. She couldn't hear her cry or scream for help. She couldn't hear her say, "I love you, Mommy." She couldn't hear her laugh or sing. She had to completely retrain Kelli in how to get her attention. Instead of *crying out* for her mother, Kelli had to learn to actually *come* to Susan and show her that she was hurt or needed something. It was a difficult and scary time for both of them.

One Sunday morning as I visited with a friend in the parking lot of the church, I saw Kelli fall down and skin her knee. She had obviously hurt herself, and her little knee was bleeding. But she didn't cry, even though her face showed the pain she felt. Instead, Kelli jumped up and frantically began looking for her mother. She ran past us and into the church, still not crying. I

61

followed her inside to see if I could help. Kelli ran through the foyer looking up into the faces of the women, still not crying.

Stooping down, I stopped her and asked, "Kelli, can I help?"

"No! I need my mama!" she said as she dashed away.

Finally she saw Susan talking to one of the students in our sign language class. Kelli ran to her mother, pulled her face down so that Susan was looking directly into her face, and *then* she began to scream and cry just like any other hurt child. But she had waited until she was actually looking into her mother's face because she knew her mom could not *hear* her cry. It was an amazing and heart-warming thing to watch.

Susan gathered Kelli into her arms and hugged her close, comforting and soothing her as any loving mother would a hurting child. Soon Kelli stopped crying and ran back outside to play with the other children, waving to her mother as she went.

Through the twenty years since then, I have often marveled at what I saw. And I've thought of how we should be like Kelli. She needed her mother. No one else would do. She wouldn't settle for anyone but her. Like Kelli, when we hurt or grieve, we can run straight into the arms of our Father, who will gather us into his divine embrace to comfort and soothe us until the hurt goes away.

Divine hugs often have human arms – a best friend's, a mate's, a parent's. And

63

because they are God's personified presence, it's okay to cry in their embrace. Through them God will comfort us, dry our tears, and send us back into the game of life . . . bruised, perhaps, but loved and not alone. We need him. No one else will do.

Reflections . . .

_____

_____

_____

_____

_____

_____

65

_____

_____

_____

_____

_____

_____

Reflections . . .

66

_____

_____

_____

_____

_____

_____

_____

_____

_____

_____

_____

_____

_____

you are

capable

You can
all thing
because
strength
you

You can do it! It's not always easy, but remember, you're not alone. You have an unlimited power source supporting you. You can do all things because I strengthen you!

Love,
The Lord Your Helper

Philippians 4:13

If you are like me, all you have to do is take a long look in the mirror, and your self-esteem drops. After all, I'm fully aware of my faults. I know all the mistakes I've made. My weaknesses and failures are ever before me.

It's no wonder that most people today struggle to keep a healthy self-image. "Self" seems so pathetic and flawed. Why should I, or anyone else, have any esteem for my *self*?

Lack of self-esteem spills over into every area of our lives. Because our images of ourselves are skewed, we *feel* incapable and useless. And because we are so strongly influenced by our feelings, we often *become* incapable. Then we walk around with a hangdog look that says to everyone else, "I'm incapable. I'm useless. I'm worth nothing. Go ahead, step on me."

In truth, this whole scenario is the result of a false image. It all began with a wrong descriptive term: *self-esteem.* I'm sure that word comes from the *Devil's Unabridged Dictionary* – he's the one who wants us to feel incapable and useless. It certainly didn't come from the Word of God.

For several years I've been searching for the right term to replace *self-esteem* in our vocabulary. I want a word that says, "I can do all things through Christ who gives me the strength." I want a word that says, "God knows that we are made of dust," but "our bodies are the temples of the living God." I want a word that shows that even though we are flawed and weak as human beings, we are strong and capable because the Holy Spirit lives and works through us. I believe that term is *soul-esteem.*

Our *selves* may be imperfect, incapable, and weak, but our *souls* are perfect, capable, and strong through brotherhood with Christ. Our souls are the image of the living God.

When I look in the mirror, I still see *self,* but I also look beyond self to my *soul.* I can finally look the real me in the eye and smile. I'm reminded of 1 Corinthians 13:12: "Now we see but a poor reflection as in a mirror; then we shall see face to face."

71

So, the next time you look at yourself in the mirror, look past the poor reflection and into the eyes of your soul. And hear Jesus whisper in your ear, "How's your *soul-esteem?*"

It seems too adventurous perhaps,
but God is able.
I have no one save the Holy Ghost
to rely upon.
My weak health and lack of ability
seem to deny me success,
but when I am weak, God is strong.
Depending upon him alone,
I go forward . . . though my eyes
are wet with tears,
I must go forward. O Lord,
fill me with the Holy Ghost.
Give me power to move the people.
Amen.

❧

Kiye Sato Yamamuro

When the storm was over,

she was still there,

hanging on to her faith

and determination.

I'm still here

The day before registration at college, Janice – a pretty red-haired freshman – arrived in town by bus. Carrying her single worn suitcase, held closed with an old belt because the clasps had broken, she walked the four miles from the Greyhound station to the campus on the east side of town.

Janice wandered around campus for a few minutes, just looking at the buildings with amazement. She couldn't believe she was really there. In spite of all the struggles in her life, she had finally made it.

Smiling to herself, Janice went to the administration building and climbed the giant staircase to the front doors. She pulled the huge oak doors open and slowly walked down the hall, taking in the sights and smells. Finally finding the right door, she straightened her skirt, brushed back her hair, and walked into the office. Pearl, long-time administrative aide to the president of the college, looked up and smiled.

"I'd like to see the president, please," said Janice with confidence.

"Won't you have a seat?" asked Pearl. "I'll just see if he's off the phone."

Soon Janice was shown into the president's office. Nervous but determined, she set her suitcase down and blurted out, "Sir, I'm here to go to school. I have my clothes and eighteen dollars. That's all. I can't go back home because I don't have enough money to get there. But I can work; I can work *hard*. And I'm capable of learning anything I need to learn. I want to go to school here more than anything else in the world. Can you help me?"

The president smiled. He was a warm-hearted, robust man who loved college kids . . . especially determined ones. "Yes, I think I can," he grinned. And help her he did, by

77

arranging financial aid, on-campus jobs, and scholarships.

That night, Janice called her mother. "Mama, I'm here. And I get to stay! I'm going to school!"

Then for four hard years, Janice cleaned food trays in the cafeteria, mopped floors in the student center, carried huge stacks of books to be refiled in the library, hauled trash out of the administration building, and did numerous other less-than-glamorous jobs. When Janice wasn't working, she was in class or studying.

78

Unlike most of us on campus, Janice didn't get to join in most of the social activities on campus. She had no free time. She didn't go to parties; she didn't date; she didn't join a social club; she didn't go to the movies on

Friday nights. She just worked and studied, studied and worked. And she smiled a lot.

"Hey, Janice, how's it going?" we'd ask.

"Great! With God's help, I'm still here!" she'd say and laugh as she scraped the food off yet another cafeteria tray.

During our senior year, the Hong Kong flu descended on campus with a vengeance. At one point, more than half the four thousand kids in school had the flu. Between her regular jobs, Janice went from room to room in her dorm, helping the nurse take care of sick girls, cleaning up after them, bringing them medicine and liquids. For two solid weeks she hardly slept.

Then, just as almost everyone was getting well, the flu hit Janice hard. In spite of Janice's protests that she had to go to work,

79

the nurse put her to bed. "But I can't *afford* to miss work," she moaned. "I need every dollar I earn to stay in school."

When the girls in Janice's dorm heard she was sick, they quickly went into action to repay her kindness. One friend reported to the cafeteria to scrape trays; one went to the administration building and hauled out the trash; another mopped the floors in the student center; and still another pulled her shift refiling books in the library. And they took turns doing it every day while Janice got well. When Janice returned to work, her time cards showed that she had worked four hours overtime during the week she was sick!

Janice and I graduated the same day. When I walked across the stage, I quietly received my diploma. When Janice walked

80

onto the stage a few minutes later, the entire student body rose to its feet and cheered (something that just wasn't done at solemn graduation ceremonies in those days). She had earned our great respect and admiration.

Amazed at the uncharacteristic cheering, the president stopped the formal procession and invited Janice to respond to her classmates at the microphone. Surprised, but happy, Janice walked to the podium, held up her diploma, and said six words: "With God's help, I'm still here!" It was a long time before the president could get the tears and cheers under control so the graduation could continue.

81

I've thought of Janice often through the years. In spite of difficulties and barriers, she accomplished her goal. She believed in her God, in herself, and in her capability to succeed. And, with God's help, she overcame the mountain of obstacles in her way. When the storm was over, she was still there, hanging on to her faith and determination.

Like Janice, we are capable of amazing things with the help of our God and our determination. We are as weak as our fear and as strong as our faith. We simply have to keep up the good fight and say with confidence, "With God's help, I'm still here!"

82

Reflections . . .

Reflections . . .

84

you are

blessed

Through my divine power, I have given you everything you need for life and godliness. Don't limit me to your previous experiences; I want to do new things in your life. My plans are far beyond your wildest dreams!

Love,
Your Faithful God

James 1:17; Ephesians 3:20
2 Peter 1:3

God is faithful to bless us with what we need when we need it. That doesn't mean he always blesses us with what we *want* when we want it. Unlike ours, God's timing is perfect, and the gifts he gives are chosen with divine wisdom and care.

We prefer to believe that blessings always come with "Yes" stamped on them. We struggle to understand how a blessing can be spelled "No." And yet, denial is sometimes the greatest blessing God can give us. His fatherly denial can prevent us from making disastrous mistakes in our lives, like a mother slapping away the hand of a toddler reaching for a hot pan.

How often do we prayerfully hound God to bless us at the time of our choosing? We tap our mental foot and think, *Well, go ahead, Lord; I'm waiting. I need that blessing right now. Could you please let that check come in the mail today?* We become frustrated when it doesn't come when we think it should, and we lapse into doubt and worry. Then we're surprised when God's blessing arrives at the precise moment it's actually needed.

Divine blessings come in small and large packages, expected and unexpected. They come through family, friends, employers, and even strangers. They come in times of joy and times of sadness. Sometimes we recognize them, and sometimes we don't.

Best of all, God can use you to bless someone else. He sends you to a sick friend with words of strength and love. He calls you to bless a stranger with a friendly smile and a helping hand. He inspires you to sing words of blessing, write words of blessing, or speak words of blessing as they are needed by the dying, the lonely, or the depressed.

A blessing is a tiny explosion of joy detonated by God. It ripples through the heart and showers the mind with divine light and hope. Haven't you felt it from time to time? You are blessed by your Father, your *Abba,* who loves you with the overflowing love of heaven. It's a legacy of joy you can pass on to others.

89

Remember the wonderful blessings

that come to you each day

from the hands of a generous

and gracious God,

and forget the irritations that

would detract from your

happiness.

❧

William Arthur Ward

Blessings are strange and

wonderful things.

They are unpredictable.

They can come from both

expected and unexpected places,

as long as we look for them

with open hearts.

the letter

Beautiful and blond, Diane had almost always gotten what she wanted in life. She even got Barry, the man of her dreams. They were happily married and were doing well together. Life was good except for one thing: They had no children.

For the first six years of their marriage, they had tried everything. Finally, the doctor told them quietly that Diane would never be able to have children. Barry took the news with courage, but Diane was shattered. Their perfect happily-ever-after story was seriously flawed.

During their seventh year together, Barry was called up by his army reserve unit and sent to Germany to fight with the Allied Forces. He was stationed in Germany for almost two years. Fortunately, he saw little action and returned home safely. For about three years, things returned to normal – until the letter arrived.

The official-looking blue envelope was from the German Immigration Department and addressed to Corporal Barry J. Sanders. Diane turned it over and wondered what was in it, but respecting Barry's privacy, she placed it unopened on his desk with the other mail.

After dinner that evening, Barry went to his office to do some work while Diane enjoyed a long, hot soak in the tub. When she came back downstairs, she found Barry standing awkwardly at the bottom of the steps with the blue envelope in his hand. From the look on his face, Diane knew something was wrong.

"What is it, honey? What's wrong?" she asked.

"Diane, there's just no easy way for me to tell you this. So I think you'd better read the letter for yourself." He handed it to her as he sank down in a nearby chair, put his head in his hands, and started to cry.

95

Dear Corporal Sanders:

We regret to inform you that Gretta Schmidt passed away on February 12 of this year from complications with pneumonia. Before her death, she contacted our office and requested that we make official arrangements for her three-year-old daughter, Ginny Schmidt, to come and live with you as her natural father. Please contact this office immediately with instructions.

96

Diane stared at the letter in disbelief. Then she looked at Barry's tear-stained face and slowly sat down on the bottom step.

"Is this true? Is this child yours?"

"Yes, I guess so."

"You have a three-year-old daughter, and you never told me?"

"I never knew it until now. It happened during the war. I'm so sorry."

Diane's world crumbled around her. Her perfect husband had been unfaithful to her. More than that, he had a child – something she could never give him – by another woman. She felt as if he had slapped her viciously across the face. She was angry. She was frightened. She was distraught.

97

Dropping the letter on the floor, Diane ran up the stairs crying and slammed their bedroom door. It was the most devastating sound Barry had ever heard. And he started to cry again.

Barry didn't go to their room that night. Instead, he spent the night in the recliner in

the den trying to decide how to put his life back together. He could hear Diane crying until the early hours of the morning. He cried, too, for his war-time stupidity, for Diane, for Gretta, and for little Ginny, who was all alone and probably scared. What was he going to do?

As dawn streamed into the den, he got up and slowly climbed the stairs. Knocking softly on the bedroom door, he opened it and went in. Diane was awake, but her eyes were swollen and red. His heart wrenched when she couldn't even look at him. Finally, he sighed heavily and sat at the foot of the bed.

"Honey, I know I've hurt you deeply, and I will regret it for the rest of my life because I love you with all my heart. I won't even try to dignify my actions with Gretta with an explanation. It was inexcusable and wrong. But, all that aside, I have to face the fact that I have a little girl who needs me. She's all alone. Gretta had no family. So, today I'm going to wire the German Immigration Department the money for Ginny's airline ticket to come and live with us. I just don't have any choice. I can only hope that you'll somehow be able to forgive me and help me care for Ginny. I'm sorry . . . so, so sorry."

Without reply, Diane turned her face into her pillow and began to sob. Barry got up from the bed and, with resignation, went down to his office to call the airlines and Western Union.

The next few days were a nightmare. Feeling totally betrayed, Diane couldn't even talk to Barry. He was bringing a

99

strange child – another woman's child –
into their house to live. Every time she
looked at that child she would be reminded
of his infidelity. She just didn't know if she
could cope with it.

While she stalked around the house,
depressed, silent, and angry, Barry quietly
fixed up the second bedroom for Ginny. He
coaxed Diane to help him, but she just
glared at him and walked out. She would
not act happy about this horrible situation.

100

On Saturday, Diane grudgingly agreed to
go with Barry to the airport to meet Ginny's
plane. When it arrived, Diane stood back in
the waiting crowd. Barry glanced back at
her and smiled a few times, but she just
stood, arms folded, with a tight-lipped
blank stare on her face.

After all the other passengers had deplaned from the Boeing 747, one of the airline attendants walked out with a blond bundle of energy in her arms. She was laughing as the little girl tickled her under the chin. Seeing Barry, the attendant said, "Are you Mr. Sanders?"

"Yes," he answered.

"Well, this is Ginny," she said with a smile. "Ginny, this is your daddy."

Ginny instantly held out her arms for Barry to take her. "Hi, Daddy. I've waited a long time to see you," she said smiling and putting her arms around his neck.

101

When Barry turned toward Diane, big tears ran down his face. He carried the blue-eyed, dimple-faced Ginny to Diane and said, "Ginny, this is Diane."

Ginny held out her arms to Diane and said, "Oh, you're so pretty! Your hair's the same color as mine. Will you be my new mother?"

Suddenly all of Diane's emotional barriers collapsed. Nothing that had happened was this child's fault. Diane gathered Ginny into her arms and held her close. "Yes, Ginny, I'll be your new mother. And I'll love you with all my heart."

"Me too!" laughed Ginny, wiping the tears off Diane's face.

102

Barry, Diane, and Ginny stood for a long time just crying and holding each other. The blessing Diane had always wanted had finally come to her. And even though it came out of sorrow, as days went by, it became the greatest blessing of joy she had ever known. She was a mother to Barry's child after all.

Blessings are strange and wonderful things. They are unpredictable. They can come from both expected and unexpected places, as long as we look for them with open hearts.

Reflections . . .

_____

_____

_____

_____

_____

_____

_____

_____

_____

_____

_____

you are

loved

You are loved! Sometimes in the midst of trials, you will feel unloved, unappreciated, alone, and abandoned. Even then, know that I am still working and will fulfill my special purpose for you. I'm right there to preserve your life and help you. My love for you lasts forever! Nothing and no one in this universe could ever stop me from loving you.

Love,
Your Father of
Unfailing Love

Psalm 138:7–8; Romans 8:35–39
Psalm 36:7

You are loved. Even if you don't always *feel* loved, you are loved. Even if you can't always *see* love, you are loved. Even when you feel alone or lonely, you are loved.

Our society dictates that we show love in specific, tangible, predictable ways – flowers, candy, love letters, rings. These are the acceptable ways of showing love. And yet, the most exciting expressions of love come in those out-of-the-ordinary, surprising, funny moments.

The problem is not that we are unloved; the problem is that we have a limited view of love's expression. We need to broaden our view. We need to improve our lovesight so we don't overlook the subtle, creative, unique ways that love comes to us.

Love behaves in many different ways. One person declares love through hard work, providing for a loved one. Another expresses love by carefully choosing a perfect gift and presenting it at just the right moment. Someone else lavishes tender and meaningful words on a beloved – perhaps in a specially chosen greeting card, a personally composed note, or an unexpected phone call. A fourth shows love through encouragement.

Love comes to you from many different sources too. Can you doubt the love in a tiny boy's handful of pansies plucked from the grumpy neighbor's flower garden? Can you deny the love in a Crayola portrait of Granddad? What mother would miss the love shown by a teenager who cleaned up his room without being prodded? And what about a friend who offers to help you with a crash project at work?

Love may show up wrapped in the funny papers and twine or exquisitely presented in glossy paper and glistening bows. It shines in silent glances from across the room. It might even come in a soft purr or the wag of a tail. It doesn't matter what form it takes, as long as it comes from the heart.

109

Even when all these ordinary kinds of love seem to fail, you are still loved extraordinarily. For God's love letter speaks gloriously to you: God loves you so much that he sent his precious only Son to lead you home to live with him forever. Oh, yes, you are definitely loved. Never doubt it.

To love and be loved
is like being warmed by the sun
from both sides.

Together Forever

She had lost her mother,

but she had found her Father once again,

And she knew she would be

loved and protected,

no matter what the future held.

the touch of love

The windshield wipers slapped away the pouring rain that blurred Lana's vision as she drove. But they couldn't wipe away the tears pouring down her cheeks. She swiped at them with one hand as she slowed her sports car in the increasing downpour. All the while, she relived the ache of the past few months.

During the frigid days of January, Lana lost the man she most loved – her dad. Someone called her away from her third-grade students to tell her that he was in the hospital, failing quickly from liver cancer. She raced home, packed a few things for a possible extended stay, and drove this same route from Texas to Oklahoma through blowing snow. She arrived just in time to say good-bye before he slipped away.

The hole left in her heart by her father's death matched the one left there only a few months earlier by her husband. He had deserted her and filed for divorce. Devastated by his caustic parting words and his flagrant affair with a neighbor, she still felt the pain and humiliation he had caused her.

In the ensuing months, Lana had become lonely and increasingly withdrawn. Her married friends left her out of their social activities, and she found the idea of getting involved with a singles' group unnerving and intimidating. So she spent most of her evenings and weekends grading papers for school or watching television at home, alone.

Then she had been dealt another blow. Her aunt had called this morning to say that her mother had suffered a heart attack and would probably not survive. Once again she found herself flying through bad weather, possibly to say good-bye to mother. "No! No!" she moaned. If her mother died, she would be completely alone. There would be no one left to love her unconditionally, no

115

one she could count on. And the thought made her go cold inside.

Lana brushed at her tears again, then turned up the speed of the wipers. The rain was falling so heavily and fast now that she could hardly make out the white stripes in the center of the road. As she topped a small rise, the wind hit with such force that it scooted her car slightly sideways on the highway, threatening to push into the bar ditch on the side of the road. Lightning split the darkened sky, and thunder seemed to rumble through her car. Lana cried out in fear.

116

She thought about pulling off the road until the storm subsided, but her overwhelming need to be with her dying mother forced her on. She just couldn't stop now.

The storm fit her mood anyway. And if she died in the storm, so what? She was going to be all alone and unloved. Who would care?

"Oh, God!" she whispered out loud, "where are you? Are you there, or have *you* left me too? Please God, protect me. Keep me safe. Do you still love me, God?"

Suddenly, Lana felt a kind hand touch her left shoulder, and a gentle warmth spread through her. Her inner chill vanished, and a peace she hadn't known in years washed over her heart. Even though she knew she was alone, the hand felt so real and reassuring that she turned her head to look beside her.

117

Of course, no one was there, but what she saw surprised her. Her own reflection in

the rain-splashed window stared back at her. And the most amazing thing struck her: she was smiling . . . really smiling.

That's when Lana knew. She *wasn't* alone, and she would *never be* alone. She was loved and would always be loved. Someone did care about her. As long as she remained in God's presence, she knew his divine love would warm and sustain her.

The next day, Lana's mom quietly joined her husband as Lana held her hand. And yet, Lana felt completely at peace. She had lost her mother, but she had found her Father once again. And she knew she would be loved and protected, no matter what the future held.

You, too, are loved by the Father who will never leave you or forsake you. You are his

118

precious child; you will be loved and protected as long as you remain in his presence.

Reflections . . .

120

121

122

_____

_____

_____

_____

_____

_____

_____

_____

_____

_____

_____

_____